Why Is Great-Grandma So Sad?

Jan 26, 2016

To Abishay

As you learn about the

Survivors, you become the

New Survivor. Keep their

memories alive!

Endorsements

As our author, Susan Heagy, vividly brings the reader through the trials and tragedy of this horrible time in the not-so-distant past, I felt a shiver from the cold wind blowing through slats in the concentration camp walls at morning roll call.

I hope that this story would be published abroad widely. We simply cannot allow people to forget that the Jews have been hunted like this in almost every century.

- Ted Pearce, songwriter, singer, co-founder and CEO of March of Life (US) & March of Remembrance (EU)

Susan Heagy has done the remarkable - a Christian writing a story about the Holocaust for Christian schoolchildren, sensitively and genuinely telling the story of one survivor in a way understandable and captivating for even the youngest reader and listener, including Jewish children and their parents. I would venture that many children who read this book will look for others and accept upon themselves the eternal lesson-commandment of the Holocaust, Never Again.

This book is a MUST HAVE, but make sure you have tissues nearby when reading it.

- Gidon Ariel, co-founder and CEO of Root-Source, Israel; author "Israel First!"

As a journalist, I read every word of it many times in the sad eyes of Hannahs, and I saw such "dolls" in the hands of Sarahs, who pass the memory of their parents to future.

 -Tamara Nersesyan, Journalist, Director TBN Israel

Susan Heagy's book, "Why is Great-Grandma So Sad?" bears the same mark as her work among the survivors, i.e. every individual survivor matters.

In Judaism it is said, that when one person's life is saved, it is as if the whole world is saved. Along this line it could be said, that if one survivor is remembered every survivor is remembered too.

 - Lars Bastrup Jorgensen, Jewish roots scholar, Denmark

Why Is Great-Grandma So Sad?

Discovering the Holocaust
Through the Eyes of a Child

Susan Heagy

ISBN Print: 978-0-9969092-0-4
ISBN eBook: 978-0-9969092-1-1
ISBN ePDF: 978-0-9969092-2-8
Library of Congress Control Number: 2015955243

1. Holocaust 2. Survivors 3. World War II 4. Concentration Camps
5. Ghetto 6. Hitler 7. Gas Chambers 8. Family 9. Great-Grandma
10. Sadness
I. Heagy, Susan II. *Why is Great-Grandma So Sad? Discovering the Holocaust Through the Eyes of a Child*

This publication is designed to provide accurate and authoritative information in regard to the subject matter covered. It is sold with the understanding that neither the author nor the publisher is engaged in rendering any type of professional services. If expert assistance is required, the services of a competent professional should be sought.

Why is Great-Grandma So Sad? may be purchased at special quantity discounts. Resale opportunities are available for sales promotions, corporate programs, gifts, fund raising, book clubs, or educational purposes for churches, congregations, schools and universities. For more information, visit http://www.ahi-il.org/resources/resellers/.

Design and layout: Lynne Hopwood
Illustrations: Emunah
Publishing Consultant: Mel Cohen, Inspired Authors Press, LLC
www.inspiredauthorspress.com
Editors: Anne Severance, Mel Cohen
Printed in the United States of America
Publisher: Yattir Publishing

To have Susan Heagy speak at your next event, live or by videoconferencing, write to susanh@ahi-il.org for booking information and details.

Preface

During WWII, the massive Nazi war machine called the Third Reich, met little resistance as it plowed across the landscape and the lives of the people of Europe. No one was exempt. Everyone was affected. But one people group was sought out for murder and extermination more than any other: The Jews. With fanatic hate and without mercy, the Jews were hunted and eliminated.

Though the characters in this story are fictional, it is also historically true. The experiences of this book were personally recounted by actual Survivors of the Holocaust. This is a combination of their horrific circumstances melded into the main characters. Unimaginable, terrible moments presented in a non-traumatic but historical context. Why?

So you, the Reader, can learn the history, absorb the experience and see the Hope.

Once you have read this story, you will be counted among the new Survivors. You will be responsible to keep history alive. Those who have experienced the Holocaust are in their final years. Their time is almost gone.

You, however, have time to protect our future.

Susan Heagy

Acknowledgements

For eleven years I have known I was to write a book about the Holocaust Survivors. After meeting them, hearing their experiences, realizing what inner strength they drew on to survive, I have been writing but doing nothing with those words. I knew more education was important for those who don't know. And I wanted to fulfill the request of these amazing people,

"Tell them not to forget us. Tell them to remember the Holocaust so it does not happen again."

Since 2004 I have been speaking where I can, sharing the Survivor's accounts and chafing at the slow progress I was making on teaching about the Shoah (Holocaust). I've been thrilled with opportunities to speak in public and private schools, churches, congregations and small groups... but I knew I needed to do more.

With the publishing of this book I yearn for people to know not just the 'what' of the Holocaust, but especially those who experienced it. I feel like I have been wandering the trails of writing and wishing and waiting for a long time. No more.

You may question what made the difference? What changed?

The answer is not what, but whom. Producing a book, bringing the message it contains to light, takes more than just the one who wrote it. It is a team effort.

First and foremost is my deep gratitude for the favor, mercy and grace of HaShem and Yeshua Messiah. This is for the People of the Book. This book is HIS creation and no other.

To my friend and the artist of these wonderful illustrations: Thank You! With extensive research, heartache, hours of drawing and an investment of her emotions, Emunah completed what was in my head. Our hearts met in this story and she somehow "saw" the characters without my description. Only God can do that.

Quite definitely, without Mel Cohen I would still be holding my manuscript and wandering that writing trail. God's timing was paramount in our connection but I am deeply grateful for the wisdom and marketing skills Mel has invested in me and in this book. May Adonai shine His blessings upon you both, Mel and Pat.

Without question, without Kathy Nicholson, this project would not have gone forward. More than a friend, a sister in the Lord, your heart, Kathy, was made for loving and giving. You have blessed me beyond measure for many years. I thank God for you.

I am grateful for the amazing and continuing support of the Abundant Hope Board, encouragement of so many precious friends and the love of my entire family.

The first to hear this story were my two youngest grandsons, Timothy and Luke. I will forever cherish the moment you two interrupted me as I read, to ask if you could buy a copy! Truly you are the ones that gave me the title of "author" before it was even published.

Contents

Sarah's a little frightened of her sad Great-Grandma

CHAPTER 1

Why is Great-Grandma So Sad?

"Mama, why is Great-Grandma so sad?"

"Well, honey, it is because of her memories of a time called the Holocaust, during a worldwide war, when Great-Grandma was just a little girl. It was a terrible time, when our people were being hunted and hurt just for being Jewish."

"Did someone try to hurt Great-Grandma, too?"

"Yes, Sarah, someone tried to hurt Great-Grandma, too. Maybe it is time for you to know about that time. Come sit with me and I will tell you how brave Great-Grandma was! It is because of her that you and I are here today."

Rebecca and her daughter, Sarah, settled into a large, comfortable chair where they could still see Great-Grandma Hannah. Sarah cuddled close to her mother, a bit anxious concerning what she was about to hear. She knew it was important not to miss a word and quietly waited for her mother to begin.

Sarah cuddled close to her mother

"It was a very long time ago when Great-Grandma was only seven years old."

Sarah's eyes were wide as she sat up and exclaimed, "Mama, that's how old I am now!"

Smiling at her daughter's reaction, Rebecca replied, "Yes, Sarah, she was just your age."

The Nazi army came into the city

Then, tugging Sarah back into her arms, Rebecca continued, "The year was 1941 and a man by the name of Adolph Hitler was in charge of a large army in the country of Germany. He taught everyone he could that the Jewish people were dangerous. He wanted to rid the world of every Jewish person, take all their belongings and money, and use it for his new government. First, he required all the Jews to identify themselves by wearing a Jewish star—our Magen David—on the outside of their clothes. Each had to be worn exactly as the local laws stated, or the person was arrested.

All Jews had to wear a star

Hitler had already begun pushing the Jewish people out of their homes and putting them in parts of cities with walls and fences, much like the barbed-wire fence out at Uncle Olaf's farm. This was called a 'ghetto.' The people were crowded together, and they were very uncomfortable. Why, a house like ours would have to hold 50 people, and you would have to give your room to a whole family!"

The ghetto was enclosed by a wall with barbed wire

Sarah's tummy felt queasy just thinking of having so many people live in their house and in her own bedroom.

"The Nazi army was taking over whole countries near their country of Germany and forcing Jews everywhere to run, hide, or be put into prisons or be slaves for their army. Everywhere, the Jews were forced to leave their homes and crowded into ghettos.

Great-Grandma and her parents, along with her two sisters and two brothers, had an apartment above the shop where her father was a tailor, making suits for men. They, along with their Jewish neighbors, were also forced to leave their home and move into one of these ghettos. They could only take enough furniture, clothes, and food to fit on one wagon. They were forced to give their business, apartment, and all the rest of their belongings as payment to a man for his help. Each person was allowed only one suitcase.

They could only fill one wagon

Can you imagine having to fill one suitcase from your room and leaving everything else behind forever? Which clothes would you pack? If you could only carry one doll, which one would you choose? As you can imagine, it was very difficult for their family."

Sarah kept quiet, thinking hard about what she would do.

"When they arrived at the ghetto, everyone went through a gate with soldiers guarding it. You could go in, but you could not come back out. Great-Grandma's family was assigned a place to live, sharing a small, old house with another family of five. They only had a kitchen and two bedrooms for seven in their family. Her father and brothers were in one and Great-Grandma, her mother and sisters were in another. There was no running water or bathroom—just a tiny shed out in the backyard for their toilet, which they had to share with all the houses nearby. It was the beginning of winter and going out to the toilet was a very cold experience!

After everyone was moved into the ghetto, the Jewish men were forced by the Nazi soldiers to build walls, closing everyone inside the guarded area. Later, people were selected to leave every day and work for the Nazi army. Great-Grandma's Papa and brothers left early in the morning and came home late at night, cold, exhausted, and hungry. They didn't get paid for their work of building roads, bridges, digging ditches, or anything else the soldiers could think of. Sometimes they worked in a factory, building weapons for the German army. The only food they were given during the day was a piece of bread and some water.

Everyone worked to help one another in the ghetto

Inside the ghetto, there was no work, very little money, and no food to purchase. People set up shops where cobblers could repair shoes or tailors could sew torn clothes; there were even little cafés for coffee and music. Someone started a newspaper. Another made the Jewish stars that were required to be worn; everyone had to buy one or make their own. There was no money to buy things; instead, they bartered (which means traded things)—maybe a potato to fix your shoes or stitch up a tear in your dress. Everyone was trying their best to keep life normal in bad circumstances. Nazi laws forbade children to attend school outside the ghetto, but inside, the teachers and parents started secret schools to make sure learning did not stop.

Food was not a problem in the beginning because each Jewish family had brought potatoes, meat, and vegetables with them when they were forced to move. They had believed it would be only a short time for them to live in the ghetto and never expected the Nazi army to close them in, not allowing anyone to buy food. But the food supplies didn't last long, and soon the food was all gone.

No one was allowed to leave the ghetto without a special pass and no food was allowed to be brought in. When the men workers would return in the evening, they were searched to see if they were bringing food in with them. If someone was found to have hidden food in their clothes, they were beaten and sometimes shot. From lack of food, the people began to get sick. . . ."

"Mama, I don't understand. How did not having enough food make them sick?" asked Sarah.

"When people do not have enough to eat, their bodies do not have the strength to fight off illness. Also, when you crowd many people into a small area, with no way to wash or stay clean, lice become a problem and people can get typhus."

Sarah interrupted her mother again. "What are lice? And what is ty-fous?"

Patiently, Rebecca answered Sarah's questions. "Lice are bugs that get in your hair and crawl on your body when you cannot stay clean. The lice bite and carry disease between people; those who are bitten can die. It is very contagious. If one person gets it, others do, too. But those who are strong enough to live through the sickness will not get it again, and can help others who are sick."

Sarah began to feel itchy just thinking about the lice.

"Did Great-Grandma get sick?"

"Yes, Great-Grandma, her mother, and one of her sisters all got typhus. She and her mother lived, but her sister Lydia was not strong enough, and died. It was a very sad and hard time for all of them."

CHAPTER 2

Begging for Food

"When their family ran out of food, it was decided that Great-Grandma would need to join the other small children who were sneaking out of the ghetto and begging for food in the market or going outside the town into the fields to look for vegetables and ask the farmers for help. Remember, no one was allowed outside the walls, so it was dangerous to do this. But her family was desperate.

Great-Grandma was afraid, but she knew her family was depending on her. This could only be done by the children who were small enough to fit through the few holes in the walls and could run fast enough. Your Great-Grandma won races at school before the war. She was a very fast runner.

Great-Grandma was a fast runner in school

Early in the morning, the children would crawl through holes in the ghetto walls or hide among the workers when they left through the gate in the morning. Some even went through the drain sewers underground to parts of the city outside of the ghetto. This last part was very dangerous because the poisonous gas that forms in the sewers could damage their lungs. Another danger was that there were so many underground tunnels, people could get lost and might never be found again.

Going through the sewers was dangerous

Great-Grandma told me of her first trip outside the ghetto and how frightened she was! With an empty sack tucked into the belt of her dress (to carry the food home), she crawled through a hole in the wall. Sticking her head out on the other side, she looked to see if there were any guards. She saw one walking in the opposite direction, carrying his rifle, only twenty feet away! She wiggled through the hole and ran as fast as she could. Suddenly, she heard a shout behind her, '*Halt!*' meaning 'Stop!' in German.

Instead of stopping, she ran as fast as her legs could carry her, ducking into alleys and weaving between the stalls in the market. The soldier could not keep up, and she left him behind. Once she knew she had lost him, she hid behind the trash bin next to the old newspaper office, breathing hard and shaking with fright. She waited for what seemed a very long time before having the courage to leave her hiding place and begin her 'job' of begging for food."

Sarah was trying hard to think of her Great-Grandma as a little girl of seven, running fast to escape the guards. Looking at her now, in the other room, all she could see was an old woman who always walked slowly and carefully.

Sarah tried to imagine Great-Grandma running

"All day, Great-Grandma wandered through the market and went to stores where her mother used to shop, begging for food to take back to the ghetto. Some people were kind, but many of them chased her away. By the end of the day, she had nine potatoes, a small bag of flour, two apples and a piece of salted beef—not much to feed a large family, but it would have to do. She knew of children that often went home with nothing to show for risking their lives. During the day, she saw some of the other children from the ghetto doing the same as she, desperately searching for food to keep their family alive. Now, it was almost dark, a good time to sneak back through the wall.

Sarah gathered anything to eat she could find

As she approached the ghetto, she hid in the shadows of houses at the edge of the wall where she had come through earlier in the day. She was expecting to return through the same hole, but when she arrived at that spot, she saw it had been closed up with new cement and rocks. A guard was standing nearby. Now she was really scared! She needed to find another place to get back into the ghetto. Returning would be more difficult, since she was carrying a sack of food, and now she was not sure where she should go. Her mama and papa would be worried because she was not yet home.

It took a long time of walking, running, and hiding while searching for another break in the wall, and it was getting hard to see in the dark. She finally found one, which was smaller and would be a tight squeeze, but she had no choice. She waited in the shadows to see if any guards were around. Not seeing anyone, she darted to the hole and began squeezing through. Pushing the sack ahead of her into the narrow space, she scraped her elbows and knees on the rough stone.

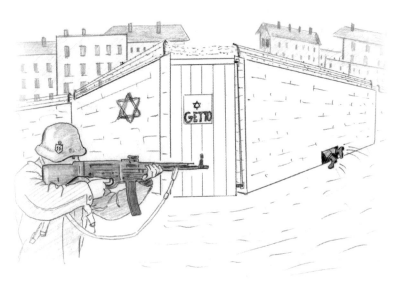

Sarah felt the sting of rock on her legs from the bullets

Suddenly she heard shouts and gunshots, the bullets hitting the ground around her legs and feet, stinging them as bits of rock broke off and nicked her skin. No longer minding the pain from the rough narrow hole, she pulled her legs and feet inside before they could shoot her. Unexpectedly, someone grabbed her hands and pulled her out to safety on the other side. A young man grinned at her in the darkness, his white teeth shining.

Sarah is surprised when she gets help

They both ran along the wall to hide between some buildings in case the guards inside the ghetto decided to look for them. The boy held out his hand for payment for helping her, and she gladly gave him two of her potatoes. Silently he disappeared into the darkness, and Great-Grandma made her way home, careful to stay in the shadows. Inside the ghetto, everyone must be off the streets before dark, or you could be arrested or even shot.

At your age, Sarah, Great-Grandma had to sneak out and beg for food three or four times a week, risking her life each time to feed her parents, brothers, and sister. Many other children as young as five years old and up to ten years of age were doing the same thing, as long as they were small enough and could run fast so they would not be caught by the Nazi soldiers."

"But, Mama," asked Sarah, "what would happen to the children if the soldiers did catch them?"

Runners ate while the rest of the family were hungry

"I don't know everything they did, but Great-Grandma did say some of her friends were hurt very badly when they were caught. It was very, very dangerous, and Great-Grandma said she was scared every day. Also, because these children were supplying the food for their entire family, they had to stay strong so they could run. The only way to do this was to give more of the food to the runners than all the rest of the family. Brothers and sisters, parents and grandparents, had such small amounts to eat; they were slowly starving while the runners ate full meals. Many of the Jewish children who were runners and lived through that time, like Great-Grandma, feel guilty even today because they had enough food and lived while some of their family members did not."

CHAPTER 3

Leaving the Ghetto

"This went on for about a year. Then, one day, the men did not leave the ghetto to work for the Nazis. For three days, they did not leave the house. Everyone was talking about an 'aktion' coming to their ghetto. Actions were when people would be taken from a ghetto to a slave labor camp or concentration camp and disappear, not returning to their families. No one knew where they went. It was a fearful time."

"Since the soldiers did not treat the people very nicely, I guess the camps were not like my summer camp," said Sarah.

"You are right, Sarah, the concentration camps were nothing like the summer camp you attended. Those camps were places where both Jewish and other people who had not broken any laws were prisoners. They were forced to work very hard with little food, and many did not live for long. In these places, the Jewish people were especially hurt.

Now, remember, the men were no longer going to work, and those in the ghetto were expecting something to change. On the evening of the third day, the ghetto police told everyone inside the ghetto to report to the main gate just before sunrise the next morning. They were told to pack one small bag to take with them. People began to ask where they were going. The answer was they would all be relocated to another place 'in the East.'

All the people were nervous. They had heard many stories about being sent 'East' and feared it meant being sent to a concentration camp. Now they had to leave everything they had brought from their house and could only take some clothes and a little food.

Great-Grandma's mama told everyone to pack two sets of clothing, a piece of soap (she divided up their one bar of soap for everyone), and gave each person a small amount of money from what she had saved and smuggled into the ghetto. They each had a small sack containing one potato, a piece of salted meat, and a turnip. The money they tucked into their underwear, carrying the food in a sack tied to their waist. When the time came to leave, everyone put on their coats, wrapped a thin blanket around their shoulders, and carried their backpack or bag. Great-Grandma had a small doll she had brought to the ghetto. She decided to take it along and tied it to her waist as well.

Great-Grandma tied her doll to her waist

As Great-Grandma and her family joined the rest of the ghetto residents in the street, they all walked to the main gate. It was quiet even though there were thousands of people walking. Hardly anyone was talking and every face showed fear. All you heard was the shuffling of feet as they walked on the old cobblestone streets. Great-Grandma held her papa's hand in a tight grip. She was scared inside, but felt better with Papa beside her. Arriving at the main gate, they saw people coming out from the different streets and gathering into one place. At the entrance, the soldiers stood around large trucks, telling the people to climb into the open back of each one. The sun was just coming up, so the bright street lights were still on, creating an eerie feeling of being between night and day.

When it was Great-Grandma and her family's turn to climb into the trucks, the soldiers were getting impatient at how long the process was taking. The soldiers began shoving people, causing them to drop their bags before climbing up, and allowing no time to retrieve them. Papa had already warned them to hold tight to their bags and to move quickly. He and her brothers climbed in first and grabbed Mama, Rose, and her, quickly pulling them up into the truck. Great-Grandma was glad her doll was tied tightly to her waist.

When their truck was packed full with everyone standing, it started up and lurched forward while the people were desperately trying to hold on and not fall out. The trip was not long, since they only went to the train station ten blocks away. They arrived with a sudden stop, causing many of the people to fall on top of one another. Great-Grandma was holding onto her papa's legs the whole way so she was not hurt. The soldiers at the station seemed to be in a hurry and were angry. They began grabbing people and throwing them to the ground. Great-Grandma's family stepped down quickly, by themselves, and joined the group. Prodded with the rifles of the soldiers, they were forced to hurry toward the train station.

Holding tight to Papa's hand and her doll

Waiting on the railroad track was the kind of railroad cars used to transport cattle. You have seen them, Sarah, when we sat in our car waiting for trains at railroad crossings. Great-Grandma saw big boxcars with wide doors in the side. The doors were open, waiting to be loaded. But instead of cows, the cattle cars were to be used for people. With no platform to climb on, everyone was pushed to climb in. However, before they could do so, the soldiers began running between them all, grabbing the bags and backpacks and throwing them to the ground. They were told they could not take their bags, 'No room!' the guards shouted. Everyone in her family was grateful for Mama's instructions to not include their food or money in their bag. It would be bad without their extra clothes, but the food and money would help in the days ahead.

It was crowded as they climbed into the boxcars

Now the soldiers began hitting them, and people were forced to climb into the cattle cars as best they could and move to the back. When the car was full, the soldiers kept shoving more and more people in. When no more people could fit into the car, the large door was slid shut, and everyone heard a lock click shut on the outside. Immediately people began to panic, pounding on the door and screaming, 'We're locked in!' Those closest tried to force the door open. No one could really move. Children and babies began to cry; men began to pray, and some of the women fainted. For several hours the train did not move. When it did, it would lurch forward, then stop, lurch forward, then stop. This went on for quite a while before the train was finally underway. It was wintertime and bitter cold. Great-Grandma was very glad for the blanket her mama had given to wrap around herself. There was one small window at the top of the car, but no other air or light came in. In the middle of the car was a bucket, the only toilet available for the approximately eighty people packed into the car."

No one knew where the train was taking them

With a deep sigh, Sarah said, "I remember when we rode on the train, Mama, but we had nice seats and windows to see out and heat in the cars. I wish Great-Grandma would have had a seat and windows, too."

"So do I, Sarah, so do I," said Rebecca softly, pausing in the telling of her story.

Great-Grandma had to hide her food

CHAPTER 4

The Arrival

"They traveled in this train for two days and two nights. No one knew where they were going . . . or why. Only one thing was for sure: The Nazis hated the Jews and did not care what happened to them. During that time, most of the people in the boxcar had no water and no food. Great-Grandma's family had their food, but had to eat it carefully so others would not see. They did not have enough to share and knew if anyone else saw it, they would take it away from them. Sometimes, when people are very hungry, they do unkind things they would not normally do. Great-Grandma felt very bad for not sharing, but knew she had no choice. Even so, without water, they were all terribly thirsty.

When the train finally stopped, the doors were not unlocked and opened for several hours. Everyone inside was thirsty and hungry, and the bitter-cold winter wind whistled through the cracks of the boxcar. The smell was terrible from the toilet bucket, and it was difficult to breathe with so many people pushed together. Suddenly, the lock rattled and the door was opened. The bright spotlights on the fences blinded the people after being in the dark for so long. They heard shouting and the words '*Raus! Schnell!*' in German. That means 'Out! Quickly!'

Papa said, 'It's a Concentration Camp.'

As the people climbed out of the boxcars down into the snow, they were told to line up. Everyone's muscles hurt from being still so long, and it was hard to move. Their clothes were not warm enough for the cold wind, and the snow blowing from the drifts hurt their hands and faces.

In front of them, they saw barbed-wire fences, tall guard houses with machine guns, and buildings inside the enclosure. Far on the other side of the clearing was a tall chimney with smoke coming out the top. Above the gate were words in German 'Arbeit macht frei.' The translation is: 'Work makes (you) free.' Great-Grandma remembers thinking this must mean her family and all the rest of the Jewish families could work and then be set free. No one knew it was a lie and their captors did not want to give any of them freedom.

Inside the gate, they could see a large open area and beyond that, many rows of long buildings. People were working in different areas, all wearing what looked like uniforms."

"Great-Grandma's papa quietly said, 'It's a concentration camp.'

The guards pushed everyone through the gate and told them to stop right inside. In front of them was a man dressed in white, holding a swagger stick. He had a smile on his face."

Sara had been fairly quiet for a long time. "Mama, what is a 'swagger' stick?"

Taking in all that her mother had to say about Great-Grandma was almost too much to hear. It was frightening to know all these things happened to her own Great-Grandma.

"A swagger stick is a lot like Grandpa's cane, Sarah, but fancier. It is not used for the reason Grandpa does—to help him walk—but is only for looks. This Nazi officer used his to decide who lived and who died by simply pointing it left or right.

Each person was told to walk toward the officer, and he would evaluate if they were strong enough to work or not. As the people began walking forward, one at a time, it soon became obvious that old men and women, babies and young children were sent to the left, and men and women who were strong enough for work were sent to the right. No children were pointed to the right, only to the left.

Of their family, Great-Grandma's papa went first, and the man pointed his stick to the right. Each of her brothers approached and was again directed to the right. Her sister Rose went next and was sent to the right. Even though they were supposed to go alone, Great-Grandma was too afraid to let go of her mama's hand. So, she and her mama went together, holding hands. The stick motioned to the left. Her mama stopped and began to argue with the man in white. He yelled at her and told her to go to the left. Great-Grandma said she had never seen her mama act like that with anyone. Not having any other choice, they both began walking to the left.

Dr. Mengele with his swagger stick

Suddenly, a fight broke out between the people still waiting and the soldiers. The officer went toward the commotion, leaving his position between the two groups already chosen. Papa yelled for Mama to run over to them. They both ran to the right side and hid in the midst of those chosen for work.

Since all the guards were watching the fighting, this change went unnoticed."

Great-Grandma and her mama run to the other line.

Sarah sat up with a puzzled look on her face and asked, "But Mama, since there were no children in that group, why didn't the guards see Great-Grandma among them?"

Rebecca smiled and gave Sarah a quick hug. "A very good question, Sarah. All through the war, there were times when people escaped, or the soldiers did not seem to see prisoners, and they experienced miracles allowing them to live. We believe they were hidden by the Hand of HaShem (God) and He protected them. I think that is what happened with Great-Grandma.

Great-Grandma told me she stood with her family surrounding her in the middle of those chosen to work. They all saw her and her mama run to them and helped them hide by standing close together.

After waiting a long time—until all the selections were made by the man in white—the soldiers now began separating the men from the women, forming new lines. The men were marched away to a different part of the camp. Two tall fences made of barbed wire with a gate kept the men's side from the women's and the main gate. As Great-Grandma watched her papa and brothers marched away, she felt more afraid than she had ever felt before.

Now the women were forced to walk quickly to the long buildings, called barracks, they had seen from outside the gate. These barracks were like large, long wooden cabins. The guards yelled at the women and hit them, ordering them to enter and choose a bed. When they got inside, they could see rows of bunk beds but with more beds on top, up to the ceiling, four layers high. It was crowded with all the women chosen to work, so Great-Grandma went with her mama and sister. Up to eight women had to sleep in each layer of one bed. The rest of the women prisoners helped hide Great-Grandma between them and got her past the guards at the doorway.

Great-Grandma hid under the mattress

Right away, before the women guards came inside, Great-Grandma was pushed inside one of the bunk beds between the wooden slats and the thin straw mattresses. There was just enough room for her and her little doll, but barely enough room to breathe. Great-Grandma stayed very still and quiet, and listened to what was happening.

Women in the camp get other shoes and dresses

Almost immediately, women guards came in and yelled at the women prisoners to line up and take off all their clothes. All of their clothes and shoes were taken away, and each woman was given a thin dress to wear and shoes that most times did not match or fit. On each dress was a different number; the guards wrote down their names and numbers. But before anyone was allowed to dress, while standing there naked, all their hair was shaved off to help keep lice away. Her mama had beautiful, long, thick brown hair, which she always wore in braids wrapped around her head. Great-Grandma had enjoyed brushing her mama's hair at night, but now it was all gone. She was shocked when she saw her mama without any hair. That night, her mama cried quietly, but Great-Grandma heard her."

Sarah remained quiet, shocked to hear of the awful things that were done to Great-Grandma and her family. She nestled a little closer to her mother, not wanting to miss anything she said.

CHAPTER 5

Survival

"Early the next morning, before the sun came up, they heard the guards outside again yelling, '*Raus! Schnell!*' The women quickly got down off the beds and ran outside. Great-Grandma heard an account of what happened from Rose later. She told of how they all had to line up in the freezing cold air without coats, standing in straight lines; no one could move. They stood for two hours while the soldiers counted them over and over to make sure all were there. This happened every morning and every evening. Sometimes, the roll call was quick, but most times it was not. Each day, someone died from the cold and were taken away.

While the women went to different work places six days a week, Great-Grandma hid for hours and hours inside the bunk bed. She said her little doll was her only friend. Since she was the only child left among all the women, everyone in that barracks did their best to hide her. She could not go outside and had to stay inside the barracks, mostly in the bed, during the day when they went to work.

Great-Grandma alone with her doll in the barracks

On Sundays, there was no work, and the women often stayed inside the barracks. On this day, Great-Grandma was able to move around more, but she still could not leave the barracks at all. Because the guards did not know she was there, and the food was rationed to each person, Great-Grandma's mama and sister must share their small rations of watery soup and bread with her each day.

For two years, Great-Grandma and her family were in this prison called a concentration camp. The women rarely ever saw the men prisoners since they were in a separate area. Sometimes, they could see them marching to or from work outside the camp, heads down, obviously tired.

During that time, everyone became thinner and thinner because they did not have enough to eat. In the mornings, they received a cup of sour coffee for breakfast. In the evenings, they were given a small piece of bread and soup that was mostly water. Sometimes a few rotten potato peels were included in the soup, and an occasional turnip would show up. Some days, there were even worms in their food, and the bread was made with ground wood in the dough."

Sarah could not be silent on hearing this and burst out saying, "Mama! How could Great-Grandma and her sister and mama eat that kind of food?!"

Sarah was shocked at what they ate in the camp

"Sometimes, Sarah, we can do things we never thought were possible. Great-Grandma and her family were doing whatever they could just to live, hoping someone would come soon to set them free.

For example, one of those things was that their toilet at night was one bucket for everyone, in the corner of the room, without even a curtain for privacy. Since Great-Grandma could not leave the building, she used that, and the women emptied the bucket for her. But everyone else used the regular toilet, which was just a large, deep hole in the ground outside. Sometimes people fell in.

Great-Grandma had to hide inside the bunk bed most of the time. It was very hard on her—not being able to go outside in the sun, having to listen carefully and to stay so still, to make sure no guards ever saw her.

The work the women of their barracks did during the day was inside a very large building filled with piles of clothes, shoes, glasses, coats, baby carriages, and more. To one side were suitcases and bags waiting to be sorted. Inside the bags were the clothes and belongings that had been taken from the Jews before leaving the ghettos or when they moved into the camps.

Rose finds the dress belonging to their sister, Lydia, who died

One evening, her sister Rose returned to the barrack very upset. She confided to Great-Grandma that while sorting clothes, she had found their sister Lydia's favorite dress, easily recognizable by the embroidered flowers, handmade by their aunt. She did not want to tell their mama because it would just make her cry. They kept it a secret between the two of them.

As for the men in the camp, sometimes they were taken to the nearby town to be slaves for the businesses there or work for the Nazi army. The soldiers forced them to work outside in the cold winter, some without shoes, even in the snow.

They did the hard work of digging ditches, building roads or barracks, burying the dead and working in the crematorium."

A crematorium

Sarah opened her mouth to ask another question, but her mother was ahead of her. "A crematorium is an oven where they burned the bodies of those who died in the camp. There were other concentration camps similar to the one Great-Grandma's family was in, but even worse. Some of them were called death camps, where they killed the Jews in showers that sprayed poison gas instead of water and then burned their bodies afterward. The chimney they saw when first entering the concentration camp was for the crematoriums. Every day, ash from the chimney fell on the camp and on the people."

Sarah shivered, "That sounds terrible. Absolutely awful."

"After two years of hiding in the bed, Great-Grandma no longer fit under the mattress very well. Even though Great-Grandma did not get much to eat, still she was growing. The women of the barracks were now afraid to continue risking their lives to hide her, so they had a meeting to decide what to do with her. They could not suddenly have an extra worker, or they would all be in trouble.

Each woman had a number on her uniform and answered to that number. No names were used by the guards and every woman had a number only. One of the women in their building had just died; she had been short and petite—about the size of Great-Grandma. Since all the women were so thin from lack of food, they all looked alike to the guards. It was decided to put the uniform of the dead woman on Great-Grandma. This way she could take her place in the roll call and work with everyone else. But now they also had to shave her head. Bribing one of the women guards, they got a razor and, while Great-Grandma cried, they shaved off her beautiful hair. There was no other way.

Great-Grandma cries after her hair is shaved

The next morning, Great-Grandma reported with everyone else for roll call and stood outside for the first time in over two years. All the women prisoners stood for two hours before being allowed to go to work. Great-Grandma was so glad to feel the sunshine again that she almost didn't mind how much her legs hurt to stand so long. She worked hard to make sure none of the women regretted letting her join them. She was ten years old now, but that did not make any difference. She had to work like an adult."

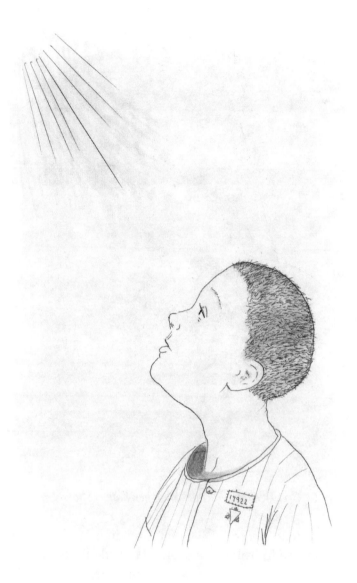

Great-Grandma enjoys the sun after 2 years in the barracks

CHAPTER 6

Liberation

"For the next six months, things were the same: roll call, coffee, work until dark, watery soup and bread, back to the barracks to share the bunk beds, eight women to a bunk. Great-Grandma, Rose, and their mama worked and ate together and shared one bunk with five other women. But Mama was getting weaker every day.

One morning when they were called to line up, Mama did not move. She had died during the night. Great-Grandma and Rose were very upset, wanted to cry and stay with her, but they could not do it. They did not have much time before roll call. Their mama had always carried a cloth bag around her neck since leaving the ghetto. When they removed it and looked inside, they were surprised to see photographs, one of which was of their mama with the two girls. They both remembered having it taken when they were in their old house. Neither of them knew their mama had been carrying this with her all along. They both began to cry as Rose hid the photographs under the mattress where they slept. They quickly wiped their tears and went out for roll call before the women prisoners carried their mama outside.

Photograph of Mama, Hannah and Rose

Now Rose and Great-Grandma only had each other. It was very hard for them to go to roll call, to work and act like nothing had happened. They were now truly alone."

"Oh, Mama!" said Sarah. "Great-Grandma's own mama died? I would cry so hard if you died!"

Rebecca gave her a quick squeeze and a sad smile.

"Over the next few months, Great-Grandma, Rose, and the other women prisoners hardly had enough strength to walk to the workroom. Then one day, they had no more work and they stayed in the barracks. No guards came to get them, and there was no roll call. Day after day, they had nothing to do. Along with no work, they received no food. After days with nothing to eat, hardly anyone was able to even get out of bed.

The Allies attack the Nazis

Then suddenly, there was an explosion near the camp. Planes began swooping low over the buildings, causing panic among the Nazi soldiers. The soldiers in the towers were shooting at the planes. When the planes stopped coming, orders were given to evacuate the camp, and all the prisoners were told to prepare to march. The guards tried to force the men and women to leave with them, but the prisoners were too weak. They had all become so thin they looked like only skin and bones.

Great-Grandma and Rose watched all this from the windows of their barracks, but they did not go outside, even when the guards shouted at them. They could barely walk anymore.

Then the planes came back, shooting at the guards. All the Nazi soldiers began to run, leaving the camp. Now it became quiet. No more planes, no more shouting guards, no shooting, just quiet. The prisoners began to slowly come out of the barracks and their hiding places. For the first time, the main gate stood open and there were no more guards. Coming down the road were jeeps and trucks, not of Nazi or enemy soldiers, but American soldiers. The camp prisoners were finally free!"

Great-Grandma and her sister Rose join the liberation

Sarah sat up with bright eyes and a wide smile. Clapping her hands, she exclaimed, "Good! Someone came to help!"

"Rose and Great-Grandma helped each other outside and stood near the gate where the soldiers entered. The soldiers were shocked! They saw what looked like living skeletons, slowly moving and walking toward them. No one had any idea how badly the Jewish people and other prisoners were mistreated.

As the prisoners came from the other side of the camp, Great-Grandma began looking for her papa and brothers. They probably would not recognize her since she was now eleven years old. Not seeing them among the men joining the soldiers, she stopped several, asking them about her papa and her brothers; did they know where they were? One man knew who she was asking about, and looked at her with a long, sad face. He touched her on the shoulder and then turned and pointed to the chimney. Without one word, she knew they were no longer alive. She and Rose truly were orphans now.

Great-Grandma understood her Papa and brothers were gone

Great-Grandma and her sister, Rose, were the only survivors of their family the day the soldiers rescued them from the camp. However, sadly, Rose died soon after their release. As the American Army and Red Cross began feeding the starved prisoners, she was one of many who were not strong enough for her body to accept healthy food. That left Great-Grandma as the only one still alive of her whole family."

Great-Grandma is sad when she remembers her family is all gone

Sarah's face registered shock as she understood what she had just heard. "Great-Grandma's whole family died? Mama, oh Mama, that is so very terrible!"

Sarah understands now why Great-Grandma is so sad

"Yes, Sarah. Great-Grandma is so sad today because it is the anniversary of when only she was set free from that concentration camp. She remembers all the terrible times and the deaths of her mama, papa, brothers, and sisters. This is a very hard day for Great-Grandma.

This terrible time is referred to as the Holocaust and must be remembered. Everyone, all people in the world, must never forget what happened to the Jewish people through the hatred of others. If we remember them and the history of what happened, we have the power to prevent it from happening again.

You, Sarah, are a symbol of life to Great-Grandma. You represent the victory she has over that horrible time. Because you are here, Great-Grandma has hope."

Getting up from the chair, Sarah gave her mother a tight hug and wiped some tears from her eyes. "Thank you for telling me about when she was a little girl, Mama. I am going to sit with Great-Grandma today and let her know I love her."

"Sarah, that is wonderful. Now that you know Great-Grandma's history, which is yours too, I think you will have more understanding of her sadness. It is hard for her to think of all she lost. However, I believe you are the best one to help her find her joy again."

Sarah turned and went in to her Great-Grandma in the next room. With a sad smile, she embraced her great-granddaughter and they began talking. Soon, Great-Grandma reached down into a cloth bag beside her on the floor. With a rustling of tissue paper, she began to carefully unwrap something, revealing it to Sarah.

Great-Grandma unwraps her doll from her time in the camp

With eyes wide, Sarah suddenly caught and held her breath. Lying in Great-Grandma's hands was a small doll, clothes torn and soiled, sparse hair matted, but with a permanent smile upon her face. Like Great-Grandma, it had survived the Holocaust. As the doll was gently placed into Sarah's hands, she let out a deep sigh, understanding the preciousness of the gift.

Great-Grandma gives Sarah her doll, and her history

With the revelation of history came the gift, and the responsibility for Sarah to be the new Survivor. She would remember her Great-Grandma's experience, and not forget it—not ever. The gifts of life, hope, and determination were now passed on to the next generation.

Mama, Hannah and Rose

Hannah as a child, age 5 before the war

Hannah's doll Rachael

Timeline

1948 May 14, 1948 Jews given State of Israel as their homeland.

1946-7 Nuremburg Trials of Nazi officers; 1 million+ Survivors homeless.

1945 Camps liberated; millions murdered, starved to death. WWII ends.

1944 Hitler deports 12,000 Jews a day from Hungary to kill in camps.

1943 Nazis send Jews on trains to camps to work for the war effort.

1942 Nazis decide on "Final Solution" to kill all Jews in Europe.

1941 Nazis attack Soviet Union; Jews murdered in camps, ghettos & villages.

1940 Nazis force Jews into ghettos, concentration camps; mass murders.

1939 WWII begins when Nazis take over countries; Jews now wear stars.

1938 "Night of Broken Glass" Jewish shops closed and burnt, Jews killed.

1937 Jews banned from all professions; Buchenwald Conc. Camp opens.

1936 Nazis boycott Jewish businesses; all Jews lose right to vote.

1935 Jews lose German citizenship and rights; persecution intensifies.

1934 Hitler takes full power as a dictator. Jewish newspapers now illegal.

1933 Adolph Hitler elected in Germany. Dachau, 1st concentration camp opens.

Glossary of Holocaust Terms

Aktion

The word referring to operations carried out against the Jews, especially in the ghettos. Usually it was for deportations to camps and killing operations.

Arbeit Macht Frei

This statement says, "Labor Makes You Free" or "Work Will Make You Free." This was at the entrance of several concentration camps to deceive the prisoners coming into the camps.

Barracks

These buildings were built like long cabins, intended for approximately 40 people to live in them. But the Nazis put upwards of 700 people in the same space. The bunkbeds built in them went to the ceiling in three or four layers sleeping up to 8 on each bed surface. Some barracks were originally built as stables for animals. They had one or two stoves to keep warm but most time the prisoners were not allowed anything to burn in them. The only toilet would be a bucket in the corner.

Boxcars

Train cars built to carry cattle were used to transport the Jews to the concentration camps. In the winter the wind came through the cracks between the boards. In the summer they were extremely hot. There was usually one very small window at the top of the car. The Nazis forced 80-100 people into each car, so tight no one could sit or lie down. Many people died on these trips.

Concentration Camp

Prisons without humane living conditions. There were

no trials or court orders for those placed there. 1932-36 they were used mostly for political prisoners. Starting in 1937 Jews and other groups unwanted by the Nazis were placed there and killed. From 1942-45 the camps were forced labor for the war effort and the Final Solution of murdering the Jews.

Crematorium

This refers to the ovens or furnaces that were built in some concentration camps to burn the murdered prisoners.

Ghetto

The first ghettos were used in 1555 to contain Jews in a certain area of a city. The Nazis used this term as they forced the Jews into the poor sections of towns, taking the homes and properties from those forced to move. Established throughout Europe these ghettos were sealed with walls and barbed wire, and guarded; no Jews allowed out. No food was allowed in, forcing starvation on the people inside. The Nazis also used the ghettos as a gathering place from which to ship large groups of people to concentration camps.

Holocaust

Derived from the Greek word *holokauston* which means *a sacrifice totally burned by fire*. The term "Holocaust" now refers to the attempted and deliberate murder of the Jewish people from 1933 to 1945. Over six million Jews were murdered during the Holocaust with many of their bodies burnt in the crematoriums.

Liberation

This is the term used when one army rescues people enslaved by another people group. Holocaust Survivors use the word to describe when they were set free from the concentration and labor camps.

Lice

A bug that gets in someone's hair and crawls on their skin, biting the person. They are often associated with unclean conditions and carry the disease of typhus. Going from one person to another in crowded conditions can cause an outbreak of typhus or other diseases.

Magen David

A six pointed star which is a symbol of the Jewish people. During the Holocaust, and in times in the past, the Jews were forced to wear the stars to identify them for purposes of persecution.

Mengele, Joseph, MD

Senior physician at Auschwitz-Birkenau Concentration Camp 1943-45. He made the selection of prisoners at the camp, as to who died and who lived. He also did experiments on prisoners.

Nazis

Name stands for National Socialist German Worker's Party. This group took control of the government in Germany. They were military based, anti-Semitic (hate Jews), racist and controlling, known for their cruelty.

Raus! Shnell!

German language meaning "Now! Quick!" Nazi soldiers used this term frequently as they forced prisoners in WWII to move fast and do what they told them.

Rollcall

Referred to as *Appell*, the prisoners were forced to stand outside in all kinds of weather, in clothes that were not warm enough in the winter. The rollcall often lasted several hours of standing. It was used for counts, punishment or selections for work details.

Runner

These were children, usually ages 5-10, that were chosen to sneak out of the ghetto to find food for their families. They needed to be fast and resourceful and brave.

Swagger Stick

This was a short but fancy cane carried by a Nazi officer. Dr. Mengele was known for using his swagger stick to direct people to live or die.

Typhus

This is a disease that usually kills those who catch it. Usually spread by lice or fleas which were common in the ghettos and the concentration camps.

Holocaust Survivor Biographies

Read about these Survivors whose personal experiences gave truth and life to this book. Their strength, intent to survive, and resourcefulness are an inspiration. From their amazing energy and true life accounts was born the personalities of those in "Why is Great-Grandma So Sad?"

Nina

In 1941 Nina with her mother, brother and sister were marched for several months from their village to a ghetto. On the way her brother was taken by the Nazi soldiers and killed. By the time they arrived in the ghetto Nina's sister and mother were ill and died soon afterward.

Nina was eight years old and now alone in the ghetto. She also became sick but did recover. Soon after that the Red Cross paid the Nazi army for Jewish children. They were taken to the train station to be sent to England, but the Russian army arrived before she could go. The Nazis and the Russians fought for several days and she was then liberated.

Klara

At the age of eight, an *aktion* was carried out on her street. Everyone was gathered into a group and shot. She was wounded, her little sister was killed and her mother was badly hurt. Klara was trapped among the dead bodies and could not get up. Her mother died and two days later Klara was found by a woman in the ghetto. She took her home to join her own eight children and took care of her.

Klara was alone now so she sneaked out of the ghetto but was caught by the soldiers. She was returned and she sneaked out again. By the end of the war she had been in three different ghettos, trying to escape.

Klara told of how hungry she was and scared. But she was also very brave and would not give up. She slept under the snow, in the forest, in the field; Klara did anything she had to in order to survive.

At the end of the war Klara found her father; they were the only two who lived from their family.

Sonya

The day the German soldiers marched into their town Sonya was four years old. But she remembers the details and how scared she was. The tanks and soldiers came down their street; the soldiers broke into houses and took what they wanted.

The Nazis formed a ghetto in her town and they were forced into it. Later the Nazis put Romanian soldiers in charge of the ghetto. These soldiers were very cruel. She recalls them stopping someone in the street in the winter and demanding their boots, making them walk away without anything on their feet.

They lived through that time by getting vegetables from the farmers outside the ghetto.

Rela

Their family was forced into the ghetto in their town. Rela and her husband had young children, two sons and one daughter. They heard about an *aktion* planned to gather all the men and kill them. That night all the men, including her husband, sneaked out of the ghetto and went into the woods to join resistance fighters there.

For a few weeks all the women in the ghetto were forced to work for the Nazis. Then one day everyone was gathered and put in boxcars to go to concentration camps. But the Nazis took all the children and babies from the mothers and put them in separate cars. Halfway to the camp the train stopped, all the children were taken out and shot in front of the mother's cars. Rela saw her three children killed and did not want to live. But she did live, surviving three concentration camps and a death march in the winter, walking through snow without shoes.

Rela shows the strength and resilience of the Survivors. She found her husband after the war and had two more sons. As of July 2015, Rela has reached the amazing age of 101 years old.

Evgenia

What she remembers most about the war was starving. When she speaks of it she cries and shakes, describing the gnawing feeling in her stomach and not able to sleep at night. For a child at that time it was very hard. Once her mother gave her a horse's hoof to chew on so she would feel a little better.

Cipora

Taken at the age of eighteen, Cipora spent seven months in a concentration camp. She saw many things, including the process they used to make soap from the human fat of those who were burned in open pits.

Though Cipora saw many horrible acts and suffered greatly, she has a sweet spirit with all who visit her. She smiles and is grateful for company.

David

As an active Zionist before the war, David lived through ghettos and three concentration camps during the war. At liberation, David returned to the Soviet Union. There, because of his Zionist beliefs, Stalin had him sent to the mines to work. He would have stayed in that place and died except for the death of Stalin six years later. At that time he was released. However, David sustained lung and hearing damage from the mine work. Even so, he is cheerful and praises God for bringing him through the war.